AF270418

TORONTO
BLUE JAYS

BY PATRICK DONNELLY

SportsZone

An Imprint of Abdo Publishing
abdobooks.com

abdobooks.com

Published by Abdo Publishing, a division of ABDO, PO Box 398166, Minneapolis, Minnesota 55439. Copyright © 2023 by Abdo Consulting Group, Inc. International copyrights reserved in all countries. No part of this book may be reproduced in any form without written permission from the publisher. SportsZone™ is a trademark and logo of Abdo Publishing.

Printed in the United States of America, North Mankato, Minnesota.
102022
012023

Cover photo: David Kirouac/Icon Sportswire/AP Images
Interior Photos: Ron Vesely/MLB Photos/Getty Images Sport/Getty Images, 4, 24, 30; Robert Reiners/Getty Images Sport/Getty Images, 6; Focus on Sport/Getty Images Sport/Getty Images, 8, 11, 12, 15; Tony Bock/Toronto Star/Getty Images, 9; Ronald C. Modra/Getty Images Sport/Getty Images, 16; Jeff Goode/Toronto Star/Getty Images, 18; Rusty Kennedy/AP Images, 19; Hans Deryk/AP Images, 21; Jeff Carlick/MLB Photos/Getty Images Sport/Getty Images, 22; Jeff Haynes/AFP/Getty Images, 27; Rich Pilling/Sporting News/Getty Images, 31; Sporting News/Getty Images, 32; John Williamson/MLB Photos/Getty Images Sport/Getty Images, 34; Mark LoMoglio/Icon Sportswire/Getty Images, 37; Tom Szczerbowski/Getty Images Sport/Getty Images, 39; Cole Burston/Getty Images Sport/Getty Images, 41

Editor: Steph Giedd
Series Designer: Becky Daum

Library of Congress Control Number: 2022940484

Publisher's Cataloging-in-Publication Data

Names: Donnelly, Patrick, author.
Title: Toronto Blue Jays / by Patrick Donnelly
Description: Minneapolis, Minnesota: Abdo Publishing, 2023 | Series: Inside MLB | Includes online resources and index.
Identifiers: ISBN 9781098290368 (lib. bdg.) | ISBN 9781098275563 (ebook)
Subjects: LCSH: Toronto Blue Jays (Baseball team)--Juvenile literature. | Baseball teams--Juvenile literature. | Professional sports--Juvenile literature. | Sports franchises--Juvenile literature. | Major League Baseball (Organization)--Juvenile literature.
Classification: DDC 796.35764--dc23

CONTENTS

LIKE FATHER, LIKE SON

Vladimir Guerrero Jr. hit his first home run in May 2019. It was exactly the kind of moment the Toronto Blue Jays had had in mind when they signed him back in 2015, when he was just 16 years old. The only question the team had at the time was how long it would take to get there.

Canadian baseball fans knew the Guerrero name well. Vlad Jr.'s dad had begun his Hall of Fame career with the Montreal Expos. He played eight seasons as an outfielder for the Expos, who have since moved to Washington, DC. But now Vlad Jr. was set to carry on the family tradition with Canada's other team. Fans watched his rise closely. By April 26, 2019,

Vladimir Guerrero Jr. became the youngest player in Blue Jays history to hit a home run at just 20 years old.

Guerrero, *left*, celebrates his first major league homer with teammate Randal Grichuk on May 14, 2019.

shortly after his 20th birthday, he was ready to make his big-league debut with the Blue Jays.

Most young hitters need an adjustment period, and Guerrero did as well. But his lasted only two weeks. On May 14, the Blue Jays visited San Francisco to play the Giants. And Toronto's young star was ready to shine.

Many fans were still finding their seats when Guerrero stepped up to the plate in the top of the first inning. Too bad for them—they missed a bit of history. Guerrero worked the count full against Giants starter Nick Vincent. Then Guerrero unleashed his mighty swing, driving a fastball 438 feet (133.5 m) to straightaway center field.

Guerrero became the youngest player in Blue Jays history to hit a home run. He was mobbed in the dugout by his teammates. Many figured this was just the first of many bombs to be unleashed by Guerrero. They didn't know the second would come later in the same game.

SAN FRANCISCO TREAT

Vladimir Guerrero Jr.'s big day in San Francisco wasn't his first time at the Giants' ballpark. Nor was it the first big power display for the family at that stadium. In 2007 Guerrero Jr. watched his father play there in the All-Star Game. He was even on the field the day before as Guerrero Sr. won the All-Star Home Run Derby title.

In the sixth inning, Vlad Jr. crushed a ball to left-center, the deepest part of San Francisco's Oracle Park. That one traveled 451 feet (137 m) and drove in Toronto's final three runs of their 7–3 victory. It also impressed someone in the other dugout who had led the Giants to three World Series titles.

"This kid, he's going to be a great player," Giants manager Bruce Bochy said. He went on to add, "You saw the bat speed, you saw how the ball comes off his bat. You better make pitches to him. I've seen his dad hit balls like that."

GREAT WHITE NORTH

Longtime Blue Jays fans surely recall a time when the team didn't have young stars such as Guerrero to lead the team. The Blue Jays began play as an expansion team in the American

League (AL) in 1977. They joined the league along with the Seattle Mariners. In doing so, the Blue Jays became the second Canadian team in Major League Baseball (MLB) history. The Montreal Expos had debuted in the National League (NL) in 1969.

Like most expansion teams, the Blue Jays struggled early on. The team stocked its first roster at the expansion draft by sorting through unwanted players from other teams. The Blue Jays did manage to grab a few quality players, however.

Toronto's first pick was utility player Bob Bailor of the Baltimore Orioles. Bailor hit .310 as a rookie. He became a regular in the Blue Jays' starting lineup for their first four years. Third baseman Garth Iorg spent nine years with the club. Catcher Ernie Whitt was a fixture in the

Versatile infielder and outfielder Bob Bailor played for the Blue Jays from 1977 to 1980.

Right-hander Jim Clancy was a consistent asset to the Toronto starting rotation for 12 seasons.

lineup throughout the 1980s. And starting pitcher Jim Clancy, Toronto's third pick, was the best of the bunch. Clancy won at least 10 games in eight of his 12 seasons with the Blue Jays.

More than 30 years later, he remained among the team's all-time leaders for games started and wins.

Toronto didn't have a classic ballpark that could host an MLB team. So the Blue Jays played their home games at Exhibition Stadium. It was a converted football stadium on the Toronto waterfront, close to Lake Ontario. Over the years, it made for some interesting playing conditions, including flocks of seagulls descending onto the field.

Of course, it was also frequently cold and windy. Gusts whipped up from the lake and sent chills through the players and fans. The first game in Blue Jays history was a perfect example of the weather challenges that Exhibition Stadium presented. Instead of opening on the road to account for Ontario's long winters, the Blue Jays opened their first season with seven straight home games. On April 7, 1977, Exhibition Stadium hosted its first baseball game. The visitors were the Chicago White Sox—and a blanket of snow. Wind chills dropped to 10 degrees Fahrenheit (−12°C). And a Zamboni was called on to clear the field.

But it was baseball, and the locals were thrilled to be a part of it. First baseman Doug Ault homered in his first two at-bats, and the Blue Jays rolled to a 9–5 victory. They finished that first homestand 5–2 and were all alone in first place. However, the bottom dropped out quickly. The Blue Jays suffered through losing streaks of eight, nine, and 11 games throughout the season and finished 54–107. Still, the Blue Jays set a record for expansion teams by drawing 1.7 million fans.

Blue Jays fans kept showing up to Exhibition Stadium the next two seasons, even though the team lost 102 and 109 games, respectively. Their original manager, Roy Hartsfield, was fired at the end of the 1979 season, although that year provided one of the franchise's early highlights. Shortstop Alfredo Griffin was named the AL Co-Rookie of the Year after hitting .287 and scoring 81 runs.

The Jays scuffled through a few more losing seasons before beginning to turn things around in 1983. They improved from 78 to 89 victories that year, setting expectations for good things to come in Toronto.

Coming off the 1979 Rookie of the Year Award, Alfredo Griffin led the majors in triples in his second season with the Blue Jays.

CHAPTER 2

THE SWINGIN' 1980s

In 1984 the Blue Jays ran into a little bit of bad luck. Looking to build off their 89-victory performance a year earlier, they started the season with six wins on a 10-game road trip. They never dropped below .500 after that. And soon they were on fire. In mid-May, they began a streak of 15 wins in 17 games, pushing their record to an impressive 34–15. Yet they were still 4 1/2 games out of first place.

That's because the Detroit Tigers began the season by winning 35 of their first 40 games. It was to the Blue Jays' credit that they stayed close to this dominant Tigers team. They used outstanding pitching to keep the pressure on Detroit. Right-hander Dave Stieb, fresh off consecutive 17-win seasons,

Blue Jays starter Dave Stieb led the AL with a 2.48 ERA in 1985.

continued to be a workhorse on the mound. He led the majors with 267 innings pitched and went 16–8 with a 2.83 earned-run average (ERA).

Stieb was part of a four-man rotation that started all but 22 games for the Blue Jays that year. Veteran Doyle Alexander went 17–6. Luis Leal and Jim Clancy each won 13 games. Meanwhile, a young group of position players continued to improve as Toronto built one of the league's top hitting attacks.

First baseman Willie Upshaw, second baseman Dámaso García, shortstop Tony Fernández, and third baseman Rance Mulliniks formed a steady, young infield. All four were between 26 and 28 years old, and each played in at least 125 games. In the outfield, George Bell led the team with 26 homers. Meanwhile Lloyd Moseby drove in a team-high 92 runs and stole 39 bases.

As good as Toronto was that year, there was no catching Detroit. The Tigers won 104

FIFTH TIME'S THE CHARM

Dave Stieb is Toronto's all-time leader in victories. He is also the all-time leader in heartbreaking close calls. Four times between 1985 and 1989, Stieb took a no-hitter into the ninth inning, only to be denied. In three of the games, he needed just one more out to complete the task. On August 4, 1989, he retired the first 26 New York Yankees he faced at SkyDome. But Roberto Kelly ruined the perfect game with a two-out double in the ninth. Stieb didn't give up, however. He finally got his first no-hitter in Cleveland on September 2, 1990.

George Bell played in Toronto for nine seasons. He earned the AL Most Valuable Player (MVP) Award in 1987, when he led the league in runs batted in (RBIs).

games and rolled to a World Series title. The Blue Jays had to settle for a second straight 89-win season and their first second-place finish. But the table was set for the boys in blue to deliver the next season.

PUTTING IT TOGETHER

Everything fell into place for the Blue Jays in 1985. The team's starting lineup remained almost entirely intact from the year before. Right fielder Jesse Barfield joined Moseby and Bell to form one of the most dynamic outfields in baseball. The trio combined for 73 home runs and 80 stolen bases. Barfield also

Lloyd Moseby slides safely into home during a 1985 game against the Kansas City Royals.

showed off a cannon for an arm, leading the league with 22 outfield assists.

On the mound, Stieb and Alexander continued to shine. Stieb won 14 games and led the AL with a 2.48 ERA. Alexander again won 17 games, while lefty Jimmy Key joined the rotation and went 14–6. One important development came in the bullpen. The Blue Jays had lacked a consistent closer for the first part of the season. That finally changed when they called up right-hander Tom Henke from the minor leagues. Henke quickly took over the closer role and saved 13 games in 14 chances down the stretch.

The Blue Jays took over first place in the AL East in mid May. They eventually stretched their lead to 9 1/2 games in early August. But the New York Yankees got hot and refused to go away. After sweeping three games against the Brewers at Milwaukee in late September, the Blue Jays led the Yankees by 5 1/2 games with just six left to play. One more win would clinch their first division title. Instead, they were swept in Detroit, allowing the Yankees to pull to within three games.

One series remained—against the Yankees at Exhibition Stadium. The division would be decided head-to-head. The Yankees needed a three-game sweep to force a one-game playoff. They got started on the right foot, rallying for two runs in the ninth against Henke to win the opener 4–3.

The next afternoon, more than 44,000 fans came out on a cool, breezy day to watch the Blue Jays try to seal the deal. Catcher Ernie Whitt, Moseby, and Upshaw hit solo homers to stake Toronto to an early 3–0 lead. Bell followed with a fourth run on a sacrifice fly. That was enough for Alexander. The veteran right-hander went the distance on a five-hitter to defeat his former team 5–1.

After setting a team record with 99 wins, Toronto hosted the Kansas City Royals in the AL Championship Series (ALCS).

Stieb pitched them to a 6–1 victory in Game 1. The next day, Al Oliver was the unlikely hero. The team had acquired the 38-year-old in a midseason trade to provide a veteran bat off the bench. On this day, he singled home the winning run in the 10th inning.

The Royals won Game 3 at home. But Oliver did it again in Game 4. This time he slashed a two-run double in the ninth inning as Toronto won 3–1. In prior years, that would have been enough to send the Blue Jays to the World Series. But in 1985, MLB expanded the league championship series from a

Righty Tom Henke led the league in saves during the 1987 season.

best-of-five to a best-of-seven format.

Still, the Jays needed to win just one of the final three games to advance. Instead, their bats went silent. The Royals held them to five runs over the last three games and clinched the series with a convincing 6–2 win in Game 7 at Exhibition Stadium.

Al Oliver slugs a two-run double to bring in the winning run in Game 4 of the 1985 ALCS.

CONSISTENTLY CLOSE

Despite the disappointing loss, the previous three seasons had established the Blue Jays as a threat in the AL East. They finished above .500 every year from 1983 to 1993 and topped 90 wins five times in that span. The 100-loss days of the expansion Blue Jays had become a distant memory.

Toronto continued to have difficulty finishing the job, however. The Jays and Tigers were close most of the 1987 season. In late September, Toronto won seven straight to take a 3 1/2 game lead with a week to play. But then disaster struck.

The Blue Jays lost their last seven games, including three straight one-run losses at Detroit to end the season. A 1–0 Toronto loss on the final day of the season gave the Tigers the AL East title.

Two years later, in 1989, the Blue Jays made a big midseason move. It wasn't a trade, however. The team literally moved across town. It left Exhibition Stadium for the spacious, ultramodern SkyDome, which featured the first retractable roof on a stadium. SkyDome also had a massive, three-story video board, a Hard Rock Cafe, and a huge McDonald's restaurant high above right field. Above center field there was even a luxury hotel.

Unfortunately, Blue Jays fans didn't have much to hold their interest once they entered the space-age ballpark. The team lost to the Brewers 5–3 on June 5 in their SkyDome debut. And in early July, the Blue Jays were scuffling along, seven games under .500 and 10 games out of first. But they turned it around, going 20–9 in August to pull into a first-place tie at the end of August, later taking first place solely on September 1. They stayed on top of the AL East the rest of the way, clinching the division with a pair of one-run wins over Baltimore on the season's final weekend.

In the ALCS, however, the Blue Jays ran into the Bash Brothers. Mark McGwire and José Canseco led the way as the

The Blue Jays played their first game in the SkyDome on June 5, 1989, in front of more than 48,000 fans.

Oakland Athletics eliminated Toronto in five games. A similar scenario played out in 1991. This time the Blue Jays won 91 games and their third AL East title. Although they split the first two games of the ALCS against the Twins at Minnesota, the Blue Jays were swept in three straight at SkyDome. And the Twins advanced to the World Series.

At this point, it would have been hard to blame Blue Jays fans for wondering if the team would ever get over the hump. Little did they know, their patience was about to pay off in historic fashion.

BLUEJAYS
GATES
13

CHAPTER 3

WORLD CHAMPIONS

The Blue Jays might have been frustrated with their postseason performance. But even the 1991 ALCS disappointment showed that the team had a lot to build on. The Blue Jays were already reaping the rewards from a trade made after the 1990 season. They sent first baseman Fred McGriff and shortstop Tony Fernández to the San Diego Padres. In return, Toronto received outfielder Joe Carter and second baseman Roberto Alomar. Carter led the team in home runs and RBIs in 1991. Meanwhile, the 23-year-old Alomar made his second straight All-Star appearance and hit .295 with 53 stolen bases. Both players would take on important roles for the Jays in upcoming seasons.

Second baseman Roberto Alomar became a key player for the Blue Jays during the early 1990s.

Slugger Joe Carter led the Blue Jays in several offensive categories during his time with the team from 1991 to 1997.

The fans rewarded the team by flooding through the gates at SkyDome all season. In 1991 the Blue Jays became the first team to draw 4 million fans to their home games. They broke that record in 1992, pushing the attendance figure to 4,028,318—or nearly 50,000 fans per game.

Those huge crowds had plenty to cheer for. In 1992 the Blue Jays were in first place for most of the season. They finished strong, winning seven of their final nine games to clinch the division title on the final weekend.

Carter again led the way with 34 homers and 119 RBIs. Forty-year-old Dave Winfield, who signed as a free agent before the season, thrived as the designated hitter (DH) with 26 homers and 108 RBIs. On the mound, Jack Morris—another free agent addition—won 21 games. Second-year righty

Juan Guzmán went 16–5 with a 2.64 ERA. And Tom Henke saved 34 games.

The ALCS was set up to be a battle with the Oakland Athletics. Both 96-win teams were hungry for postseason redemption. The A's had won four AL West titles in five years but brought home only one World Series title. Meanwhile, the Blue Jays were still looking to advance past the ALCS for the first time. Plus, they wanted revenge on the A's for their loss in 1989.

The teams split the first two games in Toronto before the Blue Jays posted a 7–5 win in Game 3. The series turned in Game 4 when Alomar came up with one of the biggest hits in team history.

The A's led 6–4 in the ninth inning and had Dennis Eckersley, the most dominant closer of his era, on the mound looking for the save. Eckersley had saved 51 games that year and would be named the AL MVP and Cy Young Award winner as the best pitcher in the league. But the Jays didn't blink. Devon White led off with a single. Alomar followed with a home run to right field to tie it. The Toronto bench erupted. The players knew opportunities for late-game rallies against the A's were rare, so they didn't waste the moment. After Alomar threw out a runner at home in the ninth inning, the Jays scratched across a run in the 11th and held on for a

7–6 win. They went on to clinch it in Game 6, as Guzmán earned his second win of the series in a 9–2 blowout. For the first time, the Blue Jays were AL champions.

BRING ON THE BRAVES

The opposing Atlanta Braves had lost a seven-game thriller to the Minnesota Twins in the 1991 World Series. They were a battle-tested group with a dynamite, young pitching staff and veteran bats throughout the lineup.

Atlanta's Tom Glavine limited Toronto to four hits in a 3–1 Braves win in Game 1. Then Atlanta appeared to be on the verge of taking a 2–0 series lead the next night. It held a 4–2 lead in the eighth inning. But Toronto's Winfield singled home a run to cut the lead in half. And in the ninth, pinch-hitter Ed Sprague launched a two-run homer to put Toronto on top 5–4. Henke wiggled out of trouble in the bottom of the ninth, and the teams headed north with the series tied at a game apiece.

Game 3 was the first World Series game ever played outside the United States. And more than 51,000 fans came out to witness history at SkyDome. Once again the Blue Jays came through with a late rally to send them home happy. Kelly Gruber's solo homer in the eighth tied the game, and Candy Maldonado's RBI single in the ninth gave Toronto a 3–2 win. The next night's game was just as close, with Toronto's

Jimmy Key outdueling Glavine 2–1.

The Blue Jays had a chance to clinch the title in Toronto, but the Braves came back with a 7–2 win. Then it was Atlanta's turn for late heroics in Game 6. Henke entered in the bottom of the ninth, trying to close out the win. But the Braves' Otis Nixon's two-out single tied the score 2–2.

That set the stage for Winfield's big moment.

Dave Winfield hits a two-run double in Game 6 of the 1992 World Series to secure the Blue Jays' first championship.

The future Hall of Famer, playing in his 19th season, had never won a World Series ring. But with two on and two out in the top of the 11th, Winfield yanked a ground ball over third base and into left field for a two-run double. In the bottom of the inning, the Braves put the tying runs on base. But Toronto's Mike Timlin retired Nixon to close out the Blue Jays' first World Series title.

BACK-TO-BACK

The Blue Jays entered the 1993 season in unfamiliar territory. As defending champions, they had a target on their backs all year long. And they had a couple of big holes to fill. Winfield moved on to the Twins as a free agent. The Blue Jays replaced him with another veteran looking for his first World Series ring. Paul Molitor had spent 15 years with the Milwaukee Brewers and made the postseason just twice. Though he was a skilled hitter, numerous injuries hampered him throughout his career. But the Blue Jays' opening at DH was a perfect fit.

The other key departure was in the bullpen. After saving 217 games in eight seasons, Henke left to sign a free agent deal with the Texas Rangers. Manager Cito Gaston handed the Blue Jays' closer role to 29-year-old Duane Ward. It wasn't a huge stretch to imagine Ward as the team's top reliever. He'd spent parts of seven seasons with Toronto and had racked up 76 saves along the way.

Both players thrived in their new roles. Ward was dominant, leading the AL with 45 saves and posting a 2.13 ERA. And Molitor led the majors with 211 hits while driving in 111 runs and hitting .332. The Jays also got a big year out of first baseman John Olerud. The 24-year-old lefty sprayed hits all over the field, leading the majors with 54 doubles and winning the AL batting title with a .363 average.

The familiar faces also contributed their consistently outstanding numbers as well. Carter blasted 33 homers and drove in 121 runs. Alomar hit .326 and stole 55 bases. And White had 42 doubles and 34 steals while winning his fifth career Gold Glove in center field.

Those six players represented the Blue Jays at the All-Star Game along with starting pitcher Pat Hentgen, who won 19 games in his first year in the rotation. Three other Toronto starters posted double figures in wins.

The race for the AL East title was competitive throughout the summer. On July 31, the Blue Jays and Yankees were tied for first. The Red Sox, Orioles, and Tigers remained in the chase, too. Toronto then made a trade with the A's to pick up veteran speedster Rickey Henderson. The MLB career stolen base leader took over the leadoff spot in the batting order. And in the final two months, he scored 37 runs while stealing 22 bases. Finally, the Blue Jays went on a tear,

PICK YOUR POISON

Opposing pitchers didn't have many opportunities for easy outs when facing the Blue Jays in 1993. When the season ended, the top three batting averages in the AL belonged to Toronto hitters. John Olerud hit .363 to become the first Blue Jay to win a batting title. Paul Molitor and Roberto Alomar finished second and third, respectively. It was the first time in 100 years that the top three hitters in the league played on the same team.

winning 16 of the final 18 games in September to run away with the division title. In the ALCS, Guzmán and Dave Stewart each won both of their starts as the Jays beat the Chicago White Sox in six games.

That set up a wild World Series between the Blue Jays and the Philadelphia Phillies. After splitting the first two games in Toronto, the Jays' bats heated up in Philadelphia. Over the next two games, they pounded out 30 hits and scored 25 runs. A 10–4 win in Game 3 put Toronto in the driver's seat. The next night, the Phillies took a 14–9 lead into the eighth. But the Jays rallied for six runs, with Henderson's two-run single and White's two-run triple giving them the lead. Ward got the final four outs, and the Blue Jays had a 15–14 victory.

Carter celebrates his three-run walk-off homer to win the 1993 World Series.

Just one win away from back-to-back titles, the Jays ran into Curt Schilling. The Phillies pitcher shut them out 2–0 in Game 5. Still, the Blue Jays had two more chances to close out the series in front of their home fans. In Game 6, the Phillies staged their own late rally to take a 6–5 lead into the bottom of the ninth.

Paul Molitor, *right*, celebrates Toronto's 1993 World Series title. He was voted the MVP of the Series.

With two runners on base, Carter stepped into history's spotlight. He lined a three-run homer to left off Phillies closer Mitch Williams. It was the first walk-off homer to win a World Series since 1960. After Carter raced around the bases, his teammates carried him off the field on their shoulders. The SkyDome crowd continued to roar long after the players had left the field. The first Canadian team to win a World Series had also become the first team to win two straight titles since 1978.

CHAPTER 4

DROUGHT AND REVIVAL

After the Blue Jays won back-to-back World Series, their fans might have thought they were watching the start of a dynasty. But those championship teams leaned heavily on veterans. And it proved difficult to replace those key players as they grew older and moved on.

The 1993 title winners began to break up immediately. Rickey Henderson went back to the Oakland Athletics after the World Series. Duane Ward suffered a shoulder injury and missed the entire 1994 season. Two of the younger stars, Roberto Alomar and Devon White, left as free agents after the 1995 season, as did Paul Molitor. John Olerud stayed on through 1996, when he was traded to the New York Mets.

Cy Young Award winners Roger Clemens, *left*, and Pat Hentgen carried the Blue Jays' pitching staff in the late 1990s.

Slugging first baseman Carlos Delgado played for the Blue Jays for 12 of his 17 MLB seasons.

Joe Carter had four more productive seasons before he left as a free agent at age 37 in 1997.

Pat Hentgen soon emerged as the staff ace. In 1996 he went 20–10, led the majors in innings pitched, and won the AL Cy Young Award. The next year, longtime Red Sox star Roger Clemens signed with the Blue Jays and revived his career. Over the next two years, he won 41 games, led the AL in strikeouts and ERA, and won the Cy Young Award both years. However, his time with the Blue Jays was later tainted after his retirement, when he was accused of taking performance-enhancing drugs. But in 1999, Clemens was still seen as a star, and Toronto traded him to the New York Yankees in exchange for three players. One of the players gained in that trade was left-handed pitcher David Wells, who made an impact with 20 wins during the 2000 season.

By the time Clemens left the team, first baseman Carlos Delgado had become the team's top slugger. From 1996 to 2004, Delgado averaged 36 homers and 114 RBIs per season. And in 2000, he led the league with 57 doubles while hitting a career-high .344.

Despite the strong individual performances, however, the Blue Jays were rarely a playoff-caliber team. In the 21 years after their 1993 World Series title, they finished at least 10 games out of first 20 times. But they did develop another star pitcher. Right-hander Roy Halladay earned his first All-Star appearance in 2002, when the 25-year-old went 19–7. The next year he won the Cy Young Award after going 22–7 and leading the majors in innings pitched. He used his sinking fastball to dominate hitters before being traded to the Philadelphia Phillies in 2009.

JOEY BATS AND THE BREAKTHROUGH

With Halladay gone in 2010, the Blue Jays discovered another way to win. They simply hit the ball over the fence, over and over again. That season nine Toronto hitters finished with at least 14 home runs, led by José Bautista's 54. The man known as "Joey Bats" had never hit more than 16 homers in a season before that. But after overhauling his swing in 2010, he became one of the most feared sluggers of the next decade.

The Blue Jays hit 257 home runs in 2010. At the time, it was the third most of any team in MLB history. They also won 85 games. Unfortunately, they were playing in the rugged AL East. The Yankees and Boston Red Sox were caught up in an arms race, regularly outspending the rest of the league in an effort to top each other. And down in Tampa Bay, the Rays had built one of the most efficient and effective organizations in the league. They used a seemingly endless line of outstanding young prospects to compete with the division's top guns.

Designated hitter Edwin Encarnación provided power at the plate for the Blue Jays for eight seasons.

But the Blue Jays persevered, and they finally broke through in 2015. Third baseman Josh Donaldson, picked up in an offseason trade with the Athletics, won the AL MVP Award after hitting 41 homers and driving in 123 runs. Meanwhile, Bautista hit 40 long balls and DH Edwin Encarnación added 39 as the Jays led the majors in runs scored.

They caught fire in the second half of the season, after trading for shortstop Troy Tulowitzki and starting pitcher

David Price in late July. An 11-game winning streak in early August lifted them from six games out of first into the top spot in the division. From there, they ran away with the division.

Price went 9–1 after the trade, and the Blue Jays won the AL East by six games.

However, the Blue Jays dropped the first two games at home in a best-of-five against the Texas Rangers in the AL Division Series (ALDS). Facing elimination, they rebounded by winning the next two in Texas. Then in Game 5 at SkyDome, Bautista broke open a 3–3 game in the seventh with a massive three-run homer. After he stood at home plate watching the flight of the ball, he flung his bat in the air before trotting around the bases. Bautista's iconic bat flip took its place beside Alomar's homer off Dennis Eckersley and Dave Winfield's World Series–winning double among huge moments in Blue Jays history.

Unfortunately, the Jays couldn't carry that momentum over into the ALCS. They lost the first two games to the Royals in

BLUE JAYS IN BUFFALO

The 2020 season was delayed by the COVID-19 pandemic. When play began in late July, the border between Canada and the United States was closed. The Blue Jays ended up playing their home games in Buffalo, New York. It proved to be a good fit for the young Jays, who went 32–28 in the shortened season and reached the playoffs before losing to Tampa Bay in the first round.

José Bautista flips his bat after hitting a three-run homer in the seventh inning of Game 5 of the 2015 ALDS.

Kansas City, scoring just three runs in the process. The Royals eventually won the series in six games, holding the Jays to three runs or fewer in all four losses.

The bats were booming again the next year, while lefty J. A. Happ went 20–4 to lead the pitching staff. The Jays won 89 games and claimed one of the two wild-card spots in the AL playoffs. In the wild-card game, Encarnación's three-run walk-off homer in the 11th inning gave Toronto a dramatic 5–2 win over the Baltimore Orioles. They faced Texas again in the ALDS, this time making quick work of the Rangers by sweeping them in three games. But once again, the bats fell silent in the

ALCS, as Cleveland held the Jays to eight runs while taking the series in five games.

YOUTH MOVEMENT

By 2018 veterans such as Bautista and Encarnación had moved on, and the Blue Jays were retooling the roster around a number of young prospects. Three second-generation MLB players debuted in 2019, led by Vladimir Guerrero Jr. at third base. Second baseman Cavan Biggio played the position held by his father, Craig, with the Houston Astros. And Bo Bichette, son of former Colorado Rockies star Dante Bichette, took over the shortstop job in the second half of the season.

By 2021 Guerrero was the main story. He moved across the diamond to play first base. That year he tied for the major league lead in homers with 48 and finished second in MVP voting. Bichette and outfielder Teoscar Hernández each made the All-Star team. And lefty Robby Ray won the AL Cy Young Award. However, the Blue Jays missed the playoffs.

Ray left as a free agent in the offseason, but the Blue Jays still improved. The team's young lineup thumped 200 home runs in 2022. Righty Alek Manoah won 16 games. The Blue Jays returned to the playoffs. Their stay was short, as they were swept in the AL Division Series. But the message was clear—the young Blue Jays were ready to contend.

Shortstop Bo Bichette led the AL with 191 hits in just his third MLB season in 2021.

TIMELINE

1977

The Toronto Blue Jays begin play as an expansion team in the AL.

1979

Shortstop Alfredo Griffin wins the AL Co-Rookie of the Year Award, though the Blue Jays lose 100 games for the third straight season.

1983

The Blue Jays post their first winning record at 89–73.

1985

Toronto edges the New York Yankees to win its first division title before falling to the Kansas City Royals in the ALCS.

1987

The Blue Jays lose their final seven games and finish second in the East to the Detroit Tigers.

1989

After opening SkyDome in June, the Jays win their second division title but lose to the Oakland Athletics in the ALCS.

1991

The Blue Jays reach the ALCS for a third time but lose to the Minnesota Twins in five games.

1992

Toronto finally reaches the World Series, then brings the trophy back home to Canada with a six-game victory over the Atlanta Braves.

1993

The Jays make it two in a row, taking down the Philadelphia Phillies in six games with Joe Carter's walk-off home run clinching the World Series at SkyDome.

1996

Pat Hentgen wins 20 games and is the first Blue Jay to win the AL Cy Young Award.

1998

Roger Clemens is the third straight Cy Young winner for the Jays as he wins his second in a row.

2003

Roy Halladay continues the strong pitching tradition in Toronto as he goes 22–7 and wins the AL Cy Young Award.

2010

Led by José Bautista's 54 home runs, the Blue Jays lead the majors in homers.

2015

Third baseman Josh Donaldson wins the AL MVP Award and leads the Jays to the AL East title. After Bautista's homer wins the ALDS over the Texas Rangers, the Blue Jays fall to the Royals in the ALCS.

2016

Toronto again reaches the ALCS, this time as a wild card, but the Jays are eliminated by Cleveland in five games.

2019

Rookies Vladimir Guerrero Jr., Cavan Biggio, and Bo Bichette follow in their fathers' footsteps and make their major league debuts.

2021

Guerrero hits 48 home runs, tying him for the most in the major leagues.

TEAM FACTS

FRANCHISE HISTORY

Toronto Blue Jays (1977–)

WORLD SERIES CHAMPIONSHIPS

1992, 1993

KEY PLAYERS

Roberto Alomar (1991–95)
José Bautista (2008–17)
George Bell (1981, 1983–90)
Joe Carter (1991–97)
Carlos Delgado (1993–2004)
Tony Fernández (1983–90,
   1993, 1998–99, 2001)
Vladmir Guerrero Jr. (2019–)
Juan Guzmán (1991–98)
Roy Halladay (1998–2009)
Pat Hentgen (1991–99, 2004)
Jimmy Key (1984–92)
John Olerud (1989–96)
Dave Stieb (1979–92, 1998)

KEY MANAGERS

Cito Gaston (1989–97, 2008–10)
John Gibbons (2004–08,
   2013–18)
Jimy Williams (1986–89)

HOME STADIUMS

Exhibition Stadium (1977–89)
Rogers Centre (1989–)
   Also known as:
   SkyDome (1989–2005)

LONG-BALL BARRAGE

On September 14, 1987, the Blue Jays set a major league record by hitting 10 home runs in an 18–3 win over the Baltimore Orioles. Catcher Ernie Whitt hit three, while outfielder George Bell and third baseman Rance Mulliniks added two apiece.

HELLO AND GOODBYE

On June 15, 2003, Blue Jays outfielder Reed Johnson had quite a day. He led off the bottom of the first against the Chicago Cubs with a home run. Then in the 10th inning, Johnson won the game with a walk-off homer. He was only the fourth player in MLB history to accomplish that feat.

SWING AND A MISS

Former Blue Jays shortstop Alex Gonzalez holds a share of a major league record that nobody wants to claim as their own. On September 9, 1998, Gonzalez struck out six times in a 13-inning loss to Cleveland. Seven other players have struck out six times in an extra-inning game, but all went longer than 13 innings.

NICE START

The Blue Jays won their first-ever game, defeating the Chicago White Sox on April 7, 1977, at Exhibition Stadium. In that game, pinch-hitter Al Woods made the game extra memorable by hitting a home run in his first major league at-bat.

GLOSSARY

ace
A team's best starting pitcher.

bullpen
The area of a baseball field where relief pitchers warm up; also used to refer to a team's relievers as a group.

closer
A pitcher who comes in at the end of the game to secure a win for his team.

dynasty
A team that has an extended period of success, usually winning multiple championships in the process.

expansion team
A new team that is added to an existing league.

free agent
A player whose rights are not owned by any team.

pandemic
A widespread outbreak of a disease that affects a large portion of the population.

save
When a relief pitcher comes in to finish a close game and secures a win.

shut out
When a team allows no runs in a complete game.

utilityman
A member of a baseball team who plays various positions in the absence of regular players.

veteran
A player who has played for many years.

walk-off
Any victory in which the home team scores the winning run in the bottom of the final inning.

MORE INFORMATION

BOOKS

Flynn, Brendan. *The MLB Encyclopedia.* Minneapolis, MN: Abdo Publishing, 2022.

Gitlin, Marty. *Baseball: Underdog Stories.* Minneapolis, MN: Abdo Publishing, 2019.

Hustad, Douglas. *Innovations in Baseball.* Minneapolis, MN: Abdo Publishing, 2022.

ONLINE RESOURCES

To learn more about the Toronto Blue Jays, visit **abdobooklinks.com** or scan this QR code. These links are routinely monitored and updated to provide the most current information available.

INDEX

ABOUT THE AUTHOR

Patrick Donnelly is a freelance writer who lives in Minneapolis, Minnesota. He has covered Major League Baseball for more than 20 years.